Eastern Painted Turtle

Eastern painted turtle care, health, diet, breeding, cages, pro's and cons and lots more included

BEN GEORGE CARRE

Copyright© 2023 Ben George Carre

Table of Contents

Introduction

Introducing the fascinating world of Eastern Painted Turtles, the unique and vibrant companions that bring joy and wonder to the world of reptile ownership. These turtles offer enthusiasts the chance to learn about the fine balance between responsible pet ownership and the complexities of caring for an aquatic friend.

We explore the fundamentals of caring for an Eastern Painted Turtle as a beloved pet in this extensive guide. From building a perfect habitat that emulates their natural habitat to comprehending their dietary requirements, we delve into the nuances of giving your painted turtle a thriving and fulfilling life.

Discover the interesting behaviors that make Eastern Painted Turtles such fascinating friends, as well as practical strategies for developing a strong bond with your aquatic buddy. We also cover important health and wellness topics, so you'll be equipped to maintain the health and well-being of your turtle.

Responsible pet ownership goes beyond the pleasures of company, therefore we examine the legal aspects of having an Eastern Painted Turtle, highlight typical problems that may occur, and offer workable solutions.

Join us as we uncover the keys to a happy and rewarding connection with these fascinating creatures, regardless of your level of experience with reptiles. This guide intends to be your go-to reference for all area of Eastern Painted Turtle care."

Chapter 1

Essentials of a Habitat: Designing the Ideal House for Your Eastern Painted Turtle

Ensuring the general well-being and happiness of your Eastern Painted Turtle depends heavily on creating the ideal home for it. We will delve into the nuances of habitat design in this in-depth investigation, going over important elements including the enclosure, lighting, heating, substrate, and decorations. You'll be well on your way to giving your painted turtle a healthy habitat by comprehending and putting these essential components into practice.

The Enclosure: A Four-Wall House

The enclosure is the cornerstone of your turtle's habitat. Choose a roomy and safe aquarium or terrarium that holds at least 20 gallons for one Eastern Painted Turtle and 10 gallons for each extra turtle. Since these turtles are semi-aquatic, it is essential to provide them with a basking place that is both land- and water-based.

Lighting: Reflecting Sunlight

Your Eastern Painted Turtle's health greatly depends on proper illumination. To simulate the natural sunshine they would receive in the wild, purchase a full-spectrum UVB light. This benefits the turtle's general health in addition to helping with calcium metabolism. Maintain a photoperiod of ten to twelve hours every day to facilitate a circadian rhythm.

Heating: Keeping the Right Temperatures

Your turtle's ability to regulate its body temperature depends on maintaining an appropriate temperature gradient. To get a basking area temperature of 85–90°F (29–32°C) and a water temperature of 75–80°F (24–27°C), use an underwater heater in conjunction with a basking light. This is similar to what they might encounter in their natural environments.

The Earth beneath their feet is the substrate.

Select a substrate that will meet your Eastern Painted Turtle's demands on land as well as in the water. For the water region, river boulders or smooth gravel are ideal; for the terrestrial portion, use a soft substrate like cypress mulch or coconut coir. This gives the turtle a cozy place to rest and permits its natural digging activities.

Water Quality: Unadulterated Living Areas

It is imperative to maintain immaculate water conditions for the well-being of your painted turtle. Purchase a high-quality water filter to eliminate contaminants, and do routine water changes to maintain appropriate levels of nitrate and ammonia. Keep an eye on the pH levels and try to keep it between 7.2 and 7.8, which is slightly alkaline to mimic their native habitat.

Décor: Establishing an Energetic Scene

Add a range of decorations to your turtle's habitat to make it more appealing. Use rocks, driftwood, and water plants to create hiding places and climbing routes. These components are vital to the mental and physical health of your turtle, in addition to improving the habitat.

Sunbathing Sanctuaries: Platforms for Basking

Give your Eastern Painted Turtle a special place to bask. You can make these with commercial turtle docks or with flat rocks. Make sure your turtle can easily reach the basking area from the water so it can effectively control its body temperature.

Enhancing the Environment: Increasing Mental Activity

Provide activities in your turtle's habitat that reflect its natural habits. To promote exploration and mental stimulation, add floating items like cork bark or toys safe for turtles. This keeps people from getting bored and encourages an active, healthy lifestyle.

Observation and Upkeep: A Vigilant Gaze

Keep a regular eye on the habitat's temperature, humidity, and cleanliness for your turtle. For best results, use a trustworthy hygrometer and thermometer. Regularly check for any indications of stress or disease, and take immediate action to resolve any concerns. A healthy atmosphere requires routine upkeep, such as replacing water and cleaning filters.

Health Factors: The Secret to Longevity

It's critical to comprehend your Eastern Painted Turtle's medical requirements. Plan for routine veterinary examinations to identify any possible problems early on.

Watch the state of their shell to make sure it stays smooth and devoid of any irregularities. Serve a well-rounded diet that includes leafy greens, live or frozen insects, and a range of commercial pellets.

In summary, a harmonious environment

To sum up, building the ideal habitat for your Eastern Painted Turtle is a fulfilling undertaking that calls for careful thought and attention to detail. You can make sure that your turtle not only survives but flourishes in its habitat by implementing the previously mentioned elements: a well-designed enclosure, proper lighting and heating, acceptable substrate, clean water, enriching decorations, and a watchful approach to health. Recall that a contented and robust turtle bears witness to your commitment as a conscientious pet owner.

Chapter 2

Comprehending the Behavior of Eastern Painted Turtles: A Guide for Owners

Building a strong bond with these fascinating reptiles requires an understanding of their behavior. This is especially true of Eastern Painted Turtles. We'll examine several aspects of their behavior in this thorough investigation, illuminating their innate dispositions, modes of communication, social inclinations, and reactions to external cues. Equipped with these knowledge, owners of pets may effectively traverse the subtleties of turtle behavior, resulting in a pleasant and enriching home space.

1. Natural Instincts: Interpreting the DNA of the Turtle

Like their wild counterparts, Eastern Painted Turtles display a variety of innate reflexes that have been molded by nature. These instincts include actions related to nesting, swimming, foraging, and basking. Comprehending these instincts enables pet owners to establish a habitat that satisfies the turtle's basic needs and promotes security and well-being.

2. Techniques of Communication: Turtles' Silent Language

Turtles may not be able to speak, but they may nevertheless express themselves through a variety of non-verbal clues. Important clues can be gained by observing their interactions with their surroundings, body language, and facial expressions. A basking turtle, for instance, might be controlling its body temperature, yet fast swimming could be a sign of agitation or discomfort. Understanding these tiny cues strengthens the relationship between owner and pet.

3. Sunbathing Rituals and Basking Behavior

An essential habit for Eastern Painted Turtles is basking. Pet owners can assess the general health and contentment of their turtles by studying their basking patterns. When a turtle basks in the sun or under a heat lamp, it helps with digestion, maintains the health of its shell, and regulates its body temperature. This important behavior is encouraged when a specific location is provided for basking, complete with suitable lighting.

4. Foraging and Eating: Turtles' Culinary Adventures

Being omnivores, Eastern Painted Turtles eat a wide variety of foods, such as tiny fish, insects, aquatic plants, and even crustaceans. It's easier for pet owners to provide a nutritionally balanced food when they understand their foraging habits. Feeding behaviors, such active hunting or searching their surroundings for food, reveal information about an animal's preferences and general health.

5. Social Tendencies: Individualistic Yet Collaborative Beings

Even though Eastern Painted Turtles live alone most of the time, there are times when they will interact with others, including during the mating season. Their social dynamics can be understood by observing how they interact with tank mates or by noticing behavioral changes in them. Several turtles can be kept apart from one another and from each other's basking places to reduce stress and possible confrontations.

6. Territorial Conduct: Protecting One's Own Turf

Turtles have been shown to exhibit territorial behaviors, especially in relation to their favorite hiding or basking sites. Owners of pets may observe protective stances such limb extension or vocalization (hissing). Stress is reduced and a peaceful living environment is encouraged when their territorial preferences are acknowledged and respected.

7. Reproduction Insights: Painted Turtles' Life Cycle

Those who are thinking on breeding Eastern Painted Turtles must comprehend their reproductive habits. It is essential to understand courtship rituals, nesting habits, and egg-laying patterns in order to establish an environment that is favorable for effective reproduction. Owners of pets should be ready to take on the duties involved in incubating eggs and raising hatchlings.

8. Reactions to the Environment: Adjusting to Change

The Eastern Painted Turtle reacts to environmental changes. Stress reactions can be triggered by abrupt changes in the lighting, temperature, or habitat configuration. In order to make sure the turtles adapt pleasantly, pet owners should make changes gradually and observe the turtles' reactions. Giving these animals a stable, well-kept environment helps them feel safe and secure.

9. Taking Care of Things: Honoring Limits

Although they might put up with mild handling, Eastern Painted Turtles usually prefer little to no interaction. Minimal handling is advised because too much stress might be harmful to their health. When approaching a turtle, proceed gently and provide appropriate body support. A healthy relationship between a pet and its owner is facilitated by an understanding of their comfort zones.

10. Modifications in Behavior: Concerns for Pet Owners

It's critical to keep an eye out for behavioral changes in your Eastern Painted Turtle to discover health problems or stress early on. Indications like sluggishness, altered eating habits, strange swimming patterns, or hostility could point to underlying issues. A higher quality of life and proactive care for your pet are guaranteed by routine observation and timely veterinary attention.

In conclusion, fostering understanding to strengthen a bond

To sum up, learning about the subtleties of Eastern Painted Turtle behavior is a fulfilling experience that strengthens the bond between pet owners and their seashell friends. Pet owners can construct an environment that meets the physical and psychological needs of these amazing reptiles by understanding their unique behaviors, deciphering their innate instincts, and recognizing their many communication techniques. A happy and fulfilling relationship between Eastern Painted Turtles and their owners can only really blossom with this knowledge.

Chapter 3

Feeding Advice: A Healthful Guide for Contented Painted Turtles

For your Eastern Painted Turtle to be healthy and happy, it is essential to provide a diet that is both balanced and nutrient-rich. We will examine the food requirements, feeding behaviors, and vital nutrients that are critical to the health of these fascinating reptiles in this in-depth investigation. You can add to the lifespan and health of your companion painted turtle by learning and using appropriate feeding techniques.

1. Diversity in Diet: The Cornerstone of a Healthful Diet

Being omnivores, Eastern Painted Turtles eat both plant- and animal-based diets. Incorporate a range of meals, such as commercial turtle pellets, leafy greens, tiny fish, insects, and even fruits in moderation, to provide a well-rounded diet. Your turtle will get all the nutrients it needs for development, vitality, and general health thanks to this varied diet.

2. Commercial Turtle Meat: An Essential Part of Your Diet

Superior commercial turtle pellets are specially designed to fulfill the dietary requirements of Eastern Painted Turtles. These pellets frequently include vital vitamins and minerals that are necessary for the growth of shells as well as general health. Make sure a sizable amount of your turtle's diet consists of pellets that are made especially for aquatic turtles.

3. Dark Leafy Greens: An Option Packed with Nutrients

Essential vitamins and minerals can be obtained by including dark leafy greens like kale, collard greens, and dandelion greens. Calcium, which is essential for keeping a strong and healthy shell, is abundant in these greens.

Switch up your greens to provide a range of nutrients and avoid food boredom.

4. Aquatic Plants: Emulation of Natural Environment

The diet of Eastern Painted Turtles in their natural habitat includes aquatic vegetation. To mimic this part of their normal eating habits, introduce alternatives such as duckweed, water hyacinth, or water lettuce. They get nourishment from these plants, but they also provide them with enrichment.

5. Protein Sources: Equilibrium Ratio of Plant and Animal Proteins

Growth and the development of muscles require protein. Serve a combination of plant-based proteins like lentils and peas with animal-based proteins like mealworms, earthworms, and tiny fish. Reaching equilibrium guarantees that your turtle gets the amino acids it needs to be healthy.

6. Insects: A Delicious Delight with Nutritious Advantages

A common treat for many Eastern Painted Turtles is insects. Mealworms, waxworms, and crickets provide flavor to their food while also offering important nutrients. But moderation is the key, since consuming too many high-fat insects might have negative health effects.

7. Fruits: Spoken Sweet Treats Occasionally

Because they contain sugar, fruits should only be given in small amounts, but they may still be a tasty and healthy part of your turtle's diet. Antioxidants and vitamins can be found in foods including melon, blueberries, and strawberries. In order to keep the water clean, remove any uneaten fruit right away.

8. Adapting Feeding Frequency to Age and Size

Depending on their size and age, Eastern Painted Turtles have different feeding schedules. Adult turtles can be fed every other day, but younger turtles need to be fed more frequently—typically once a day. In order to avoid overfeeding, which can result in obesity and other health problems, adjust the portion sizes appropriately.

9. Supplementing with Calcium: Forming Sturdy Shells
For a painted turtle's shell to develop and remain in good condition, calcium is essential. Although a balanced diet ought to supply enough calcium, extra supplements can be required, particularly for developing turtles and females laying eggs. You can ensure sufficient consumption by dusting food products with calcium supplements.

10. Hydration: Why Fresh Water Is So Important
Having access to fresh, clean water is just as important as having food. Make sure there is a shallow water area

in your turtle's habitat where it may soak and drink. Digestion, the health of the shell, and general wellbeing all depend on proper hydration. To keep the water at its best, clean and refill it frequently.

11. Feeding Methods: Promoting Organic Activities

Use feeding methods that promote your Eastern Painted Turtle's natural activities. For instance, use feeding tongs to provide a more hands-on experience or scatter food items in the water to pique the curiosity of potential hunters. This gives your turtle cerebral stimulation in addition to physical activity.

12. Observation and Modifications: Optimizing the Diet

Observe your Eastern Painted Turtle on a regular basis to see how it behaves and how healthy its shell is. Adapt the diet to their specific needs and any shifts in their level of activity. See a reptile veterinarian to treat any health problems if you observe weight increase, hunger decrease, or other strange behaviors.

13. Seasonal Aspects: Adjusting to Shifts in the Environment

Seasonal variations in the diet and activity levels of Eastern Painted Turtles may be observed. They might eat less during the colder months or go into a phase of decreased activity. Recognize and honor their innate cycles by adjusting feeding schedules and keeping an eye on their behavior.

14. Possible Health Concerns: Pet Owners Should Exercise Caution

Watch out for any indications of possible dietary-related health problems, such as vitamin deficiencies, shell deformities, or metabolic bone disease. Preventive care consists of regular veterinarian exams, a balanced food, and good husbandry techniques.

Concluding Remarks: Fueling a Content and Robust Turtle

To sum up, feeding your Eastern Painted Turtle is more than just giving them food; it's also about creating a varied, high-nutrient diet that mimics their dietary preferences. You support your painted turtle companion's general health and pleasure by offering a range of foods, keeping an eye on feeding schedules, and making adjustments in response to specific needs. Recall that a healthy and happy member of your reptile family is a well-fed turtle.

Chapter 4

Health & Well-Being: Taking Good Care of Your Painted Turtle

It takes more than just routine maintenance to keep your Eastern Painted Turtle healthy and happy. We will examine several facets of turtle health in this thorough investigation, including wellness in general, typical health issues, veterinarian care, and preventive measures. You may create a happy and healthy companion for your painted turtle by being aware of the nuances involved in providing for its health.

1. Preventive Interventions: The Basis for Turtle Health
The key to preserving the health and well-being of your Eastern Painted Turtle is prevention. Your turtle's general health is influenced by establishing a routine for appropriate habitat care, feeding it a balanced diet, and

providing enough sunlight and warmth. Maintaining good cleanliness and making routine observations reduces the likelihood of health problems.

2. Veterinary Care: Establishing a Bond with a Veterinarian Specialized in Reptiles

For the long term health of your Eastern Painted Turtle, it is imperative that you establish a relationship with a skilled veterinarian for reptiles. Plan on routine examinations, particularly for juvenile turtles, to track development and identify any health issues in advance. Proactive veterinary care guarantees prompt intervention and suitable treatment.

3. Shell Health: An Indicator of General Health

An Eastern Painted Turtle's shell serves as both a barrier and a gauge of its general well-being. Check the shell frequently for any irregularities, such as discolouration, soft areas, or cracks. These symptoms may indicate dietary inadequacies, metabolic bone disease, or shell rot. Robust shell health is facilitated by adequate calcium in the diet, appropriate lighting, and a clean environment.

4. Weight Management: Harmonizing Diet and Exercise
It's critical to keep an eye on your turtle's weight in order to spot any possible health issues. A healthy turtle is fat, but obesity can cause a number of complications, including difficulties with the organs. To keep your Eastern Painted Turtle at a healthy weight, be sure to feed them a balanced diet, give them the right amounts of food, and engage in frequent exercise.

5. Taking Care of Respiratory Issues in Respiratory Health
Eastern Painted Turtles may have respiratory problems, particularly if their habitat is very moist or chilly. To prevent respiratory infections, make sure that there is

enough ventilation and that the environment is kept warm and dry. Wheezing, nasal discharge, and difficult breathing are indications of respiratory distress. In the event that respiratory problems are noticed, immediate veterinary care is important.

6. Preventing Parasites: Defending Against Insects Both Inside and Outside

The health of your Eastern Painted Turtle may be threatened by both internal and external parasites. Frequent veterinary fecal investigations aid in the identification and management of intestinal parasites. to keep the habitat clean, guard against external parasites, and make sure newly added plants or tank mates are parasite-free.

7. Behavioral Observations: Recognizing Typical Trends

Recognizing any health problems in your Eastern Painted Turtle requires an understanding of its typical behavior.

Activity levels, feeding patterns, or basking preferences that change could indicate underlying issues. Keep a regular eye on your turtle's behavior, and if you see any unusual behavior, look into it more or consult a veterinarian.

8. Maintaining Clean Environments for Well-Being Turtles

Infections can be avoided and overall health can be enhanced by keeping the environment clean and hygienic. To stop bacterial growth, clean the enclosure on a regular basis, filter the water, and take out any uneaten food. A well-kept habitat ensures a healthier living environment by lowering the danger of skin and shell illnesses.

9. Reducing Environmental Stressors to Manage Stress

Stress affects turtles, especially Eastern Painted Turtles. Reduce stress by creating hiding places, keeping the surroundings stable, and preventing abrupt changes in the temperature or illumination. Turtles are more prone to sickness because stress can weaken their immune systems.

10. Temperature Control: Upholding Ideal Conditions

Being ectothermic, Eastern Painted Turtles depend on outside sources to control their body temperature. Make sure the water temperature stays in the range of 75–80°F (24–27°C) while the basking area achieves the proper temperature range of 85–90°F (29–32°C). Maintaining a steady temperature is essential for healthy metabolism, digestion, and general wellbeing.

11. Managing Aspects: Reducing Tension During Communication

Although handling turtles should be kept to a minimum, there are situations in which interaction is required, such as during health examinations or habitat management. To reduce stress, handle your Eastern Painted Turtle gently and provide appropriate body support. Handling them roughly or frequently can make them anxious and have a bad effect on their health.

12. Aging and Lifespan: Making appropriate adjustments to care. While older turtles benefit from a well-maintained habitat and regular checks for age-related health issues, younger turtles may need more frequent feedings and special dietary considerations for growth. A longer and healthier lifetime is a result of providing care that is tailored to individual life stages.

13. Veterinary Emergencies: Identifying Them and Acting Quickly

Learn about the typical symptoms of disease or discomfort that Eastern Painted Turtles may exhibit, such as changes in eating, irregular swimming, or lethargy. Having a first aid package designed specifically for reptiles and understanding the safest way to take your turtle to the vet can make all the difference in the world in an emergency situation.

14. Supplemental Nutrition: Improving Health with Dietary Guidance

Under the supervision of a veterinarian, adding dietary supplements to your turtle's food can improve its general health. Supplements containing calcium, vitamin D3, and multivitamins may be advised to meet certain dietary requirements and advance optimal health.

In conclusion: Developing a Lifelong Bond

In summary, maintaining the health and well-being of your Eastern Painted Turtle requires a comprehensive and enduring dedication. You can improve the general health of your turtle by adopting preventive measures, developing a rapport with a reptile doctor, and remaining aware of its behavior. A happy and healthy

Eastern Painted Turtle guarantees a rewarding and long-lasting friendship with these amazing reptiles, in addition to enriching your life.

Chapter 5

Developing a Relationship with Your Eastern Painted Turtle

Developing a close relationship with your Eastern Painted Turtle is a fulfilling experience that calls for tolerance, comprehension, and a sincere dedication to attending to the special requirements of these amazing lizards. We will cover a wide range of bonding topics in this in-depth investigation, such as habitat interaction, feeding schedules, enrichment activities, handling issues, and the importance of providing your Eastern Painted Turtle with a safe and trusting environment.

1. Comprehending Turtle Behavior: The Basis of Linkage

It's important to comprehend Eastern Painted Turtle behavior before starting the bonding process. Gaining a grasp of their preferences, reactions to stimuli, and social tendencies is the first step towards establishing a mutually understanding connection. Turtles may not show obvious signs of affection, but they do show subtle signs of trust and comfort.

2. Interaction with Habitat: Promoting a Cozy Environment

Interact with your Eastern Painted Turtle in its natural environment. Take time to see how it behaves when it's swimming, exploring, or basking. By getting to know it and making yourself comfortable in its living area, you build trust. Allow the turtle to become used to your presence without feeling threatened by sitting calmly close to the enclosure.

3. Feeding Customs: Establishing Favorable Connections

You have a great chance to deepen your relationship with your Eastern Painted Turtle during feeding time. Using feeding tongs or dropping food into the water, feed the animals in a regular and methodical manner. With time, your turtle will come to identify you with good things, which will help it develop a sense of trust and dependability.

4. Activities for Enrichment: Activating the Mind
Provide enrichment activities that honor the innate desires of your Eastern Painted Turtle. Add floating items to the habitat, like toys safe for turtles or cork bark. This promotes exploration and interaction in addition to offering cerebral stimulation. Like many other creatures, turtles flourish in environments that provide possibilities for interaction.

5. Regular Presence: Building Trust Through Habit
Establishing trust with your Eastern Painted Turtle requires consistency. Keep up a consistent schedule for interaction, feeding, and habitat upkeep. Turtles value consistency and predictability, which makes them feel

safe and comfortable in their surroundings. Your turtle might grow accustomed to you over time and even come over to investigate.

6. Taking Care of Things: Honoring Limits

Although different turtles have different thresholds for handling, it's important to honor their limits. Generally speaking, Eastern Painted Turtles might not be as interested in personal contact as a dog or cat. Handling should only be done sparingly and gently to prevent stress. Observe their body language; if they appear uncomfortable, it's best to leave them alone.

7. Positive Reinforcement: Honoring Credible Conduct

Use strategies for positive reinforcement when interacting with others. Give your Eastern Painted Turtle extra treats and vocal praise when they behave in ways that show they trust you, including coming over to you or accepting food from your hand. The perception that your presence is linked to good experiences is strengthened by this encouraging feedback.

8. Observational Bonding: Value of Unique Characters

Each Eastern Painted Turtle is distinct, possessing distinct characteristics and inclinations. Just observe your turtle for a while, making note of its routines, locations that it like to hang out, and responses to various stimuli. By developing the bond between you, observant bonding enables you to recognize and comprehend your turtle as an individual.

9. Establishing a Trust-Based Environment to Promote Security

Creating a safe haven for your Eastern Painted Turtle is essential to building trust. Make sure the environment satisfies their psychological and physical requirements. Provide them a clean, well-kept enclosure, a basking area, and hiding places. Your turtle gains confidence in a safe setting, making them feel comfortable with you.

10. Gradual Engagement: Letting Turtles Determine the Tempo

Respecting the speed at which your Eastern Painted Turtle bonds, let the process develop gradually. It could take some time for turtles to get used to new situations and changes. When adding new components to their environment or trying to handle them, go cautiously. It takes patience to make your turtle feel safe and at ease.

11. Grooming and Shell Upkeep: Establishing Care to Foster Trust

Bonding rituals might include grooming and shell maintenance. Examine the cleanliness and appearance of any anomalies on the shell of your Eastern Painted Turtle with gentle hands. To get rid of the debris, use a soft brush or cloth. When given in a calm and stress-free manner, this hands-on care can strengthen your bond with your turtle.

12. Honoring solitude: Recognizing personal needs

Typically, Eastern Painted Turtles live alone. They may converse and display signals of curiosity, but they also cherish their alone time. Recognize your turtle's need for seclusion and give them places to hide away from prying eyes. Maintaining a harmonious and courteous relationship requires a balance between social interaction and times of alone.

13. Speaking Together: The Influence of Calm Conversation

Even while Eastern Painted Turtles might not react to vocal cues the same way that mammals do, bonding can nevertheless occur when moderate and constant vocal interaction is provided. Over time, the link between you and your turtle will become stronger when you speak to it in a soothing and quiet manner.

14. Recognizing Territorial Behavior: Handling Limits

Turtles, such as the Eastern Painted Turtle, have the ability to act in a territorial manner. Recognize their limits and refrain from overly entering their personal space. Building trust and security in your relationship requires you to acknowledge and honor their territorial inclinations.

15. Lifelong Friendship: Adjusting to Development and Change

Your bond's dynamics may change as your Eastern Painted Turtle develops. As your turtle's needs change, modify the way you engage with him or her and the way you take care of him. To create a happy and long-lasting relationship, lifetime bonding entails a commitment to continual observation, understanding, and modification.

In conclusion, a lasting relationship

To sum up, developing a close and lasting relationship with your Eastern Painted Turtle requires mutual respect, tolerance, and understanding. You may build a relationship that improves the quality of life for both you and your turtle friend by interacting positively, providing a safe haven, and attending to each turtle's unique needs. Your Eastern Painted Turtle's lifelong bond with you is evidence of how fulfilling proper reptile care can be.

Chapter 6

Activities for Enrichment: Maintaining Your Turtle's Stimulation and Contentment

Your Eastern Painted Turtle's well being depends on you providing an environment that is both interesting and enriching for it. We will explore a range of enrichment activities in this thorough examination that support the innate instincts and behaviors of these fascinating reptiles. By adding enrichment activities, you may provide your Eastern Painted Turtle with all it needs for a happy and healthy existence, from habitat improvements to mental and physical stimulation.

1. Comprehending Enrichment: A Comprehensive Method

The goal of enrichment for Eastern Painted Turtles is to improve their entire quality of life by creating a dynamic and interesting environment, which goes beyond simple entertainment. Boredom is avoided and natural behaviors are encouraged via enrichment activities, which excite both the physical and mental elements.

2. Enhancements to the Habitat: Replicating the Natural Environment

The cornerstone of enrichment is a thoughtfully constructed setting. Build a varied habitat by adding elements like rocks, driftwood, aquatic plants, hiding places, and basking areas. These features provide possibilities for exploration, sunbathing, and refuge while imitating the natural habitat of Eastern Painted Turtles.

3. Floating Items: Promoting Organic Activities

Introduce floating items into the habitat's aquatic section. Opportunities for climbing, basking, and exploring can be found using cork bark, toys suited for turtles, or floating platforms. These items satisfy the turtle's innate curiosity and need to engage with its surroundings in addition to encouraging physical activity.

4. Feeding Difficulties: Creating Adventures Out of Meals
Implement feeding challenges to turn mealtimes into engaging activities. To encourage your Eastern Painted Turtle to hunt and explore for food, scatter food items throughout the area. This gives them mental and physical stimulation while simulating their natural foraging behaviors.

5. Live Prey and Insects: A Delectable and Engaging Delight
As a way to enrich your turtle's diet, include live prey like insects. In addition to offering a nutritional boost, earthworms, mealworms, and crickets arouse predation instincts. Observing your Eastern Painted Turtle interact

with live prey gives their daily routine a dynamic and interactive touch.

6. Mirror Reflection: Social Interaction and Curiosity

To foster curiosity and social tendencies in Eastern Painted Turtles, place a non-breakable mirror in their habitat to create the illusion of a "turtle companion." The turtles may interact with their reflection by swimming, bobbing their heads, or even "communicating." This enrichment activity is straightforward but powerful.

7. Playing in the Water: Promoting Natural Swimming Behaviors

Establish a shallow water area with different depths to promote water play and swimming. Because Eastern Painted Turtles are semi-aquatic, giving them an area to practice their natural swimming habits promotes mental and physical stimulation.

8. Environmental Shifts: Innovation and Adjustment

Periodically alter the habitat's surroundings. This could entail changing the water level, adding new components, or even altering the decorations. Changes bring novelty, which piques the interest of your Eastern Painted Turtle and encourages it to investigate its surroundings.

9. Auditory Stimulation: Soft Background Noise

Turtles don't have particularly good hearing, but they can benefit from mild background noises like running water or relaxing music. This makes the habitat more calming and stimulating, which enhances your turtle's sense of wellbeing.

10. Outside Enclosures: Sunlight and Environment

If the weather permits, think about putting your Eastern Painted Turtle in an outside enclosure. A comprehensive enrichment experience is enhanced by exposure to external elements, exposure to sunlight, and the sensation of natural substrate. Make sure there are spaces that are both shaded and exposed to sunlight within the outdoor enclosure.

11. Puzzle feeders: Engaging the Mind While Eating

Purchase puzzle feeders made specifically for turtles. Food is dispensed gradually by these systems, so your Eastern Painted Turtle will have to learn how to get to the delights. Puzzle feeders make feeding more mentally stimulating by testing their capacity for problem-solving.

12. Tactile Enrichment: Various Textures and Substrates

Provide the habitat a range of substrates with various textures. Textural enrichment is enhanced by rough surfaces for sunbathing, soft ground for digging, and smooth river rocks. Eastern Painted Turtles investigate and engage with these textures, creating a dynamic environment and appealing to their senses.

13. Making Cozy Retreats with Handmade Hideouts

Use safe resources such as hollow logs, PVC pipes, and coconut shells to create your own DIY hideouts. These hiding places are comfortable havens that provide your Eastern Painted Turtle a feeling of seclusion and safety. They can select different regions according to their wants or mood because there are a number of hiding sites.

14. Movement of Water: Replacing Natural Currents

Incorporate soft water flow in the habitat's aquatic area. A filter with an adjustable flow rate or a submersible water pump can do this. By simulating natural currents, you may get your turtle to swim more and interact with a dynamic aquatic environment.

15. Changing Seasons: Adjusting to Organic Cycles

Adjust the habitat's seasonality to conform to the cycles of the natural world. This could entail adding themed decorations, modifying temperature gradients, or changing lighting patterns. Your Eastern Painted Turtle lives in a dynamic and ever-changing habitat because to seasonal fluctuations.

16. Social Engagement: Restricted Conversations with Turtles

Although Eastern Painted Turtles are not naturally gregarious creatures, they can benefit socially from restricted encounters with other turtles in their enclosure. Make sure there is enough room for each turtle to have its own territory and that interactions are observed.

17. Known Aromas: Presenting Secure Aromas

Add safe and non-toxic fragrances to the environment, like herbal essences or fragrances suitable for aquatic life. Due to their great sense of smell, turtles can benefit from the introduction of various scents, which will enhance their surroundings.

18. Seasonal Décor: Themed Accentuation

As the seasons change or holidays approach, add festive décor to the environment. This could contain non-toxic flora, ornaments that are acceptable for aquatic environments, or themed surfaces. Your Eastern Painted Turtle will find visual stimulation and an engaging habitat with themed décor.

19. DIY Projects for Collaboration: Using Your Ingenuity

Take part in group do-it-yourself projects to make enrichment materials. This might be creating platforms that float, creating a maze that is friendly to turtles, or creating interactive elements for the environment. Using your imagination gives the enrichment process a unique touch.

20. Interactive Playthings: Encouraging Engagement

Examine engaging interactive toys that are safe for turtles. To stimulate both the mind and the body during playtime, include floating balls, puzzle toys, or treat-dispensing objects. Turn the toys around every so often to keep them interesting.

In summary, a vibrant and energetic companion

To sum up, enrichment activities are essential to improving your Eastern Painted Turtle's quality of life. You may create a dynamic and engaging atmosphere by incorporating a variety of activities that accommodate their natural habits. In addition to being healthy, a vibrant and active turtle is also more involved and satisfied in its surroundings. Maintaining a rich and stimulating environment will help your Eastern Painted Turtle develop a lasting friendship. Regularly evaluate and modify enrichment activities to make the experience exciting and fun.

Chapter 7

Typical Obstacles: Handling Problems in Eastern Painted Turtle Maintenance

Although taking care of Eastern Painted Turtles can be a fulfilling experience, there are certain difficulties involved. For the sake of your shelled companion's health and wellbeing, it is imperative that you handle these issues quickly and efficiently. We will examine the typical problems Eastern Painted Turtle owners encounter in-depth in this investigation, including advice on prevention, diagnosis, and suitable remedies.

1. Controlling Temperature: Juggling Heat and Light

A common problem in the care of Eastern Painted Turtles is establishing and preserving the ideal temperature balance in the habitat. Because they are ectothermic, turtles must rely on outside factors to control their body temperature. Inadequate basking temperatures may cause fatigue, gastrointestinal distress, and general health problems.

Preventive measures include purchasing a heat lamp or basking lamp that is dependable and produces the required temperature gradient. To maintain a water temperature of between 75-80°F (24-27°C), periodically check the temperature using a thermometer to make sure the basking area reaches 85-90°F (29-32°C).

Solution: To attain the required temperature range, modify the heat source's power and placement. If you want to control heat output and avoid overheating, think about installing a thermostat.

2. Balancing Nutrition: Fulfilling Dietary Requirements

Eastern Painted Turtles require a well-balanced diet to remain healthy. Nutritional abnormalities can cause shell deformities, metabolic bone disease, and other health problems. Examples of these include inadequate calcium intake or an excessive dependence on particular foods.

Prevention: Provide commercial turtle pellets, dark greens, aquatic plants, insects, and occasionally fruits as part of a varied and nutritionally balanced diet. When necessary, dust food items with calcium supplements; this is especially important for developing turtles and females laying eggs.

Solution: If you think there may be a nutritional imbalance in your reptile, speak with a veterinarian. They might suggest suitable dietary changes or supplements to make up for particular inadequacies.

3. Shell Health Concerns: Avoiding and Handling Shell Issues

An essential component of caring for Eastern Painted Turtles is shell health. If hygiene is neglected or the turtle is exposed to inappropriate conditions, problems including shell rot, infections, or injuries may arise.

Prevention: Keep the habitat tidy, supply enough UVB lighting for a basking area to support the health of the shell, and make sure the water is routinely purified. Steer clear of sudden changes in the environment since this could stress the turtles and affect the health of their shells.

Solution: See a reptile veterinarian right away if you see any abnormalities on the shell, such as discolouration, soft patches, or sores. Topical treatments, habitat modifications, or addressing underlying health issues may all be part of the treatment plan.

4. Keeping an Eye Out for Signs of Distress in Respiratory Infections

Respiratory diseases can affect Eastern Painted Turtles, particularly if their environment is very moist or chilly. Wheezing, nasal discharge, and difficult breathing are all signs of respiratory problems.

Preventive measures include keeping the environment dry, warm, and well-ventilated. Steer clear of abrupt temperature and humidity fluctuations. Make sure the turtle can reach its ideal body temperature in the basking area.

Solution: See a veterinarian specializing in reptiles if symptoms of respiratory distress are noticed. They might suggest making changes to the environment, controlling the temperature, or prescribing drugs to treat respiratory problems.

5. Infestations of Parasites: Consistent Monitoring and Prevention

The general health of Eastern Painted Turtles can be impacted by both internal and external parasites. Finding and treating parasite infections requires routine monitoring through fecal exams.

Precaution: Before releasing newly acquired turtles into an established habitat, quarantine them. Maintain the cleanliness of the habitat and make sure that any live prey or plants brought to the enclosure are parasite-free.

Solution: See a veterinarian specializing in reptiles if you suspect a parasite infection. If parasites are detected by fecal exams, suitable medicine can be provided for treatment.

6. Reducing Stress-Related Problems: Environmental Stressors

Stress affects turtles, especially Eastern Painted Turtles. Environmental stressors can affect an animal's health and well-being, such as abrupt changes in temperature, illumination, or handling.

Preventive: Limit handling to only those chores that are truly necessary. Provide hiding places, keep the surroundings constant, and refrain from making abrupt changes to the habitat. Keep an eye out for indicators of stress, such as behavioral or dietary changes.

Solution: Find the cause of the stress and deal with it if problems related to stress are noticed. Make sure the turtle's home is steady and make adjustments gradually so it may get used to the new surroundings.

7. Not Enough Hydration: Making Sure You Have Access to Fresh Water

For Eastern Painted Turtles to be healthy, they must drink enough water. A lack of access to clean water can cause dehydration, which can affect organ performance and general health.

Prevention: Make sure the habitat has a place with shallow water for soaking and drinking. Make sure the water is fresh and changed frequently. Keep an eye out for symptoms of dehydration, such as fatigue or sunken eyes.

Solution: See a veterinarian specializing in reptiles if you suspect dehydration. In addition to addressing any underlying medical conditions that may be causing dehydration, they can offer advice on appropriate hydration techniques.

8. Overgrown Nails and Beak: Consistent Upkeep

Eastern Painted Turtles may have overgrown beaks and nails, which can be problematic, particularly in captivity where natural wear may be restricted.

Preventive measures include giving the habitat a hard surface, like a stone, to aid in the beak and nails wearing down naturally. Keep a regular eye on their length and state.

Solution: See a reptile veterinarian if you see any overgrowth of nails or beaks. In order to encourage natural wear, they can safely trim the beak and nails and offer advice on how to improve the surroundings.

9. Managing Stress: Reducing the Effect of Interactions

Although some turtles can handle quite a bit, excessive or rough handling can lead to stress and have a detrimental effect on health.

Precaution: Handle the turtle as little as possible and only engage it when absolutely essential. Treat the turtle with care and provide it the assistance it needs. Keep an eye out for symptoms of stress, such as hissing or retracting limbs.

Solution: Decrease the frequency of handling and make sure that interactions are brief and mild if symptoms of handling-related stress are noticed. Give the turtle enough time to heal and get comfortable in its surroundings.

10. Insufficient Lighting: Encouraging Sufficient UVB Radiation

Eastern Painted Turtles may develop metabolic bone disease and other health problems as a result of inadequate UVB light exposure.

Preventive measures include using UVB bulbs made specifically for reptiles and making sure the habitat is adequately covered. Adhere to suggested lighting schedules in order to ensure appropriate exposure.

Solution: See a veterinarian specializing in reptiles if symptoms of metabolic bone disease, such as softening of the shell, are noticed. To correct calcium inadequacies, they might suggest dietary modifications and changes to the lighting arrangement.

11. Breeding Difficulties: Ethical Breeding Methods

Challenges with controlling reproductive activities, producing eggs, and raising hatchlings may emerge for owners thinking about breeding Eastern Painted Turtles.

Prevention: Be ready to take on the duties involved with breeding, such as establishing appropriate nesting places, keeping an eye on the development of eggs, and tending to hatchlings. Think about if breeding is a good fit for your experience and availability.

Solution: See an experienced breeder or a reptile veterinarian for advice if problems occur during the breeding process. Conscious breeding methods put the health and welfare of the participating turtles first.

12. Seasonal Modifications: Getting Used to Shifts

Seasonal variations in behavior and activity levels are possible in Eastern Painted Turtles. It is essential to their wellbeing that they comprehend and adjust to these seasonal shifts.

Prevention: Make seasonal modifications to the habitat's lighting, temperature, and features. Recognize the seasonal variations in natural behaviors, such as wintertime activity reduction.

Solution: Evaluate whether any observed behavioral changes are consistent with typical seasonal patterns. If you have questions concerning odd behavior patterns, speak with a veterinarian that specializes in reptiles.

Finally, a Holistic Approach to Addressing Care Issues

In conclusion, managing typical issues with Eastern Painted Turtle care necessitates a proactive and comprehensive strategy. Preventive care, timely detection of possible problems, and routine observation all help to the general health and welfare of these amazing reptiles. Building a relationship with a veterinarian that specializes in reptiles is highly beneficial, as they can offer advice, diagnosis, and treatment when necessary. Through knowledge and awareness of the special requirements of Eastern Painted Turtles, you may overcome obstacles and guarantee a happy and long-lasting relationship with these amazing animals.

Chapter 8

Legal Aspects: Handling Ownership Regulations for Painted Turtles

Although having a painted turtle—especially the Eastern Painted Turtle—is a fulfilling experience, there are certain legal issues to take into account. We will examine rules, permits, and appropriate practices to guarantee legal compliance and the welfare of these fascinating reptiles in this thorough examination of the legal implications of owning painted turtles.

1. Legal Variability: Comprehending Local Laws

The ownership of painted turtles is subject to a varied legal environment that varies greatly throughout regions. Prospective turtle owners should learn about and comprehend the unique laws and rules that apply to them, whether they are local, state, federal, or municipal. The legality of purchasing and retaining painted turtles may be impacted by laws pertaining to the ownership, importation, and trade of animals.

2. Status of Protected Species: Identification of Conservation Issues

Because of conservation efforts, some painted turtle species, like the Eastern Painted Turtle, may be protected or listed as species of concern. Native populations are frequently protected from overexploitation, habitat degradation, and other dangers by this precaution. It is imperative to identify the species of painted turtles and determine whether any restrictions pertaining to conservation are applicable before obtaining one.

3. International Trade Considerations under the CITES Regulations

An international agreement known as the Convention on International trading in Endangered Species of Wild Fauna and Flora (CITES) was created to make sure that trading in wild plants and animals would not jeopardize their survival. Certain species of painted turtles might be protected by CITES, meaning that there would be tight restrictions on their commerce. When making a foreign acquisition, prospective owners should be aware of CITES regulations and secure the required permits.

4. Local Wildlife Laws: State and Local Statutes

Ownership of wildlife is governed by laws in many nations, and even within nations, states and provinces may have their own laws. These laws may address the kinds of animals that are acceptable for pet ownership, permission needs, and captivity rules. To prevent legal problems and protect the painted turtle's wellbeing, it is imperative that you are aware of and abide by these local laws.

5. Requirements for Permits: Obtaining Legal Authorization

It could be legally necessary to get permission in some areas in order to keep a painted turtle. Usually given by departments or agencies responsible for wildlife, permits may include fees, an application process, and adherence to certain requirements. It is advisable for potential owners to obtain and verify any required permissions before purchasing a painted turtle.

6. Comparing Captive-Bred and Wild-Caught: Legal Consequences

Legal ramifications may arise from the painted turtle's origin, whether it comes from wild capture or captive breeding. Due to worries about the effects on natural populations, owning wild-caught turtles may be restricted or even forbidden in many countries. In the pet sector, captive-bred turtles are frequently preferred for moral and environmental grounds.

7. Adopting Pets Responsibly: Upholding Moral Principles

Responsible pet ownership goes beyond legal issues and entails upholding moral principles for the care and welfare of the painted turtle. This entails giving the turtle a suitable environment, food, medical attention, and a dedication to meeting its long-term requirements. A happy and moral experience for the owner and the pet is ensured by knowing the particular needs of the Eastern Painted Turtle and following best practices.

8. Specialized Permits for Scientific or Educational Use

For scientific or educational reasons, people or organizations may occasionally try to keep painted turtles. Such activities may require specialized licenses or permits. These licenses frequently include extra obligations, such outreach to educate the public or following research protocols.

9. Exotic Pet Trade: Issues and Rebuttals

The trade in exotic pets, which includes painted turtles, has come under fire because of worries about animal welfare, conservation, and the possible introduction of non-native species into new areas. To address these issues, some areas may have more stringent laws governing the purchase and ownership of exotic pets, such as painted turtles.

10. Fines and Confiscation as Legal Remedies for Violations

Regulations pertaining to wildlife violations may result in harsh legal repercussions, such as fines, pet seizure, or other sanctions. Owners of painted turtles have an obligation to remain aware of and abide by applicable legislation in order to keep out of trouble legally and support the preservation of local wildlife.

11. Conservation Projects: Aiding in Preserve Initiatives

Owners of painted turtles can take proactive steps to ensure the survival of their species by supporting or participating in local conservation programs. This could be working as a volunteer for groups that protect animals, contributing to habitat restoration efforts, or taking part in citizen science programs.

12. Raising Awareness and Advocating for Responsible Ownership

In order to affect regulatory decisions and to shape public opinion, advocacy and awareness campaigns can be extremely important. Owners of painted turtles can make a difference by encouraging responsible pet ownership, teaching others about the unique requirements of painted turtles, and lobbying for laws that strike a balance between conservation and responsible pet ownership.

13. Working Together with Authorities: Establishing Beneficial Connections

Owners of painted turtles can benefit from building strong contacts with appropriate agencies and wildlife authorities. In order to maintain compliance with current regulations, this cooperation may entail asking for advice on legal requirements, taking part in educational initiatives, and encouraging open communication.

14. Legal Updates: Remaining Up to Date on Any Changes

Regulations pertaining to wildlife may alter throughout time to reflect advancements in science, shifting public objectives, or changes in public opinion. Owners of painted turtles need to keep up with any modifications or changes to the law that can affect their ownership and modify their activities accordingly.

15. Rehoming Considerations: Ethical and Legal Considerations

When it becomes essential to rehome a painted turtle, owners need to be aware of the ethical and legal ramifications. Finding a suitable and legal home for the turtle is a necessary part of responsible rehoming, as some areas may have particular rules governing the transfer of ownership for certain species.

In conclusion, a comprehensive strategy for owning painted turtles

Taking care of a painted turtle requires more than just giving it basic care; it also entails handling legal issues and making sure that all applicable laws are followed. Owners of painted turtles support conservation efforts, ethical pet ownership, and good relations with wildlife authorities by being aware of and abiding by local, national, and international laws. The painted turtle and its owner can have a happy and long-lasting experience if a comprehensive strategy that incorporates legal knowledge, ethical behavior, and a dedication to conservation ideals is implemented.

Chapter 9

Reproduction Insights: Examining the Eastern Painted Turtle Life Cycle

The elaborate and intriguing reproduction cycle of Eastern Painted Turtles is a reflection of the species' adaptation to both land and aquatic settings. We will examine every phase of the life cycle of the Eastern Painted Turtle in detail, covering everything from mating and courtship to egg-laying, incubation, and the initial phases of hatchling development.

1. Sexual Dimorphism: Differentiating Between the Sexes

Eastern Painted Turtles exhibit sexual dimorphism, with men and females differing in specific morphological traits. Adult males frequently have longer and thicker tails, slightly concave plastrons (the lower half of the shell), and significantly smaller overall sizes than females, however these changes may not be noticeable at first. These characteristics are essential to reproductive behaviors and processes.

2. Complex Rituals for Mating and Courtship

When they are more active in the spring and early summer, Eastern Painted Turtles participate in complex courtship rituals. Males approach females and engage in visual displays, such as head bobbing and forelimb extension, to initiate courtship. In order to engage in successful courtship, the male must position himself on the female's back while submerged and use his large claws to grasp her firmly.

3. Copulation: Special Copulatory Process

Among turtles, the copulatory technique of Eastern Painted Turtles is unique. Using his lengthy tail, the male can move under the female's shell and line up his cloaca with hers. In turtles, the cloaca is a multifunctional aperture that serves digestive, urinary, and reproductive purposes. Fertilization can begin when sperm from the male can go to the female due to this alignment.

4. Selecting the Best Sites for Laying Eggs in Nests

After a successful mating attempt, females begin an important part of the reproductive process: choosing a suitable nest site for laying eggs. The Eastern Painted Turtle is well-known for its terrestrial nesting practices; it prefers sandy or loamy soils that drain well and are near bodies of water. A crucial instinct that affects the effectiveness of egg incubation and the survival of hatchlings afterward is nest choosing.

5. The Egg-Laying Process: A Careful Operation

Egg-laying by Eastern Painted Turtles is a meticulously planned activity. Depending on the age and size of the female, she will use her hind limbs to dig a flask-shaped nest cavity and deposit a varied number of eggs—usually between 4 and 15 eggs per clutch. When the eggs are placed, the female carefully shoves earth into the nest so that very little remains of it.

6. During the Incubation Period: Environmental Factors

The temperature is one of the many environmental elements that affects the incubation period of eggs laid by Eastern Painted Turtles. In contrast to several other reptiles, the temperature at a crucial stage of embryonic development determines the sex of painted turtle hatchlings rather than genetic determinants. In general, females are produced by warmer temperatures, whereas males are produced by lower temps.

7. A Novel Mechanism for Temperature-Dependent Sex Determination (TSD)

Temperature-dependent sex determination (TSD), a process seen in certain reptiles, is present in Eastern

Painted Turtles. Variations in temperature during the middle part of the incubation period affect the gender of the growing embryos. This temperature sensitivity shows the species' susceptibility to climate change and emphasizes how crucial it is to preserve appropriate breeding habitats.

8. Hatching: The Hatchlings' Emergence

Once the eggs have been incubated for 60 to 90 days, the painted turtles are prepared for hatching. An egg tooth, a transient, pointed feature on the upper jaw, is used by hatchlings to crack open the eggshell. This is the beginning of the emerging phase, and it's called pipping. After hatching, the newborn turtles spend a brief time in the nest where they can absorb the yolk sac, which supplies nutrition for their early development.

9. Nest Predation: Difficulties in Surviving Hatchlings

For Eastern Painted Turtle hatchlings, the time from hatching to entering the safety of the water is a dangerous one. A serious risk is nest predation, when a variety of predators—such as birds, animals, and other reptiles—seek out nests in the hopes of finding food. Hatchlings rely heavily on their innate behaviors to survive, including as sprinting for water and dodging predators.

10. Following Hashing: Seeking Cover in the Sea

After hatching, Eastern Painted Turtle hatchlings follow the light reflection on the water's surface to find the closest water source. Since water offers the turtles protection from predators and access to their major habitat, this activity is essential to their survival. Only a small percentage of hatchlings will make it safely from the nest to the water. The trek is dangerous.

11. Development and Growth: Infancy in Aquatic Environments

Hatchling Eastern Painted Turtles live in aquatic environments until they are in the protection of the water. They grow and mature quickly, becoming less susceptible hatchlings and more adept juveniles at navigating their environment. A turtle's ability to thrive depends on its ability to find enough food, housing, and sun-bathing possibilities, all of which are found in aquatic environments.

12. Sexual and Maturational Development: The Path to Adulthood

The sexual maturity of Eastern Painted Turtles is contingent upon several factors, including growth rates, environmental conditions, and resource availability. Males typically mature earlier than females. Changes in behavior, such as a greater emphasis on courtship and mating behaviors, are indicators of sexual maturity.

After reaching sexual maturity, Eastern Painted Turtles participate in the cycle of reproduction to ensure the survival of their species.

13. Lifespan and Longevity: Evidence of Adaptability

Like many other kinds of turtles, the Eastern Painted Turtle has an amazing lifespan. They can live for several decades in the wild, with lifespans that frequently surpass 20 years. The species' resilience and enduring existence in ecosystems are facilitated by their reproductive techniques and capacity to adapt to a variety of conditions.

14. Conservation Factors: Preserving the Success of Reproduction

The condition of their environments has a significant impact on the life cycle of Eastern Painted Turtles. Contributing to the overall success of the species are conservation activities that safeguard nesting locations, preserve conducive settings for incubation, and mitigate dangers to the survival of hatchlings. Additionally, conservation efforts are essential in reducing the negative effects that pollution, habitat loss, and climate change have on Eastern Painted Turtles and their life cycle.

15. Impact of Humanity: Juggling Recognition and Preservation

Although many people find Eastern Painted Turtles to be visually stunning and possess unusual characteristics, human actions might unintentionally affect their life cycle. Nesting locations and aquatic environments are threatened by urbanization, pollution, and habitat modification. Achieving a balance between human appreciation and the preservation of these amazing turtles requires responsible stewardship, habitat conservation, and public education.

In summary: A Life Tapestry

Eastern Painted Turtles' life cycle is a complex web of survival, adaptation, and procreation. Every stage of the life cycle, from complex courtship customs and temperature-dependent sex selection to the delicate hatchlings' hazardous voyage to water, demonstrates the species' adaptability and capacity to survive in a variety of settings. In addition to demonstrating the Eastern Painted Turtle's successful evolutionary path, knowledge of and appreciation for its life cycle serves as a call to action for conservation and responsible handling of these fascinating reptiles.

Chapter 10

Introducing Several Eastern Painted Turtles into a Habitat to Help Them Socialize

It is a complicated process to bring several Eastern Painted Turtles into one shared environment; aspects to be carefully considered include the turtles' size, behavior, and sex as well as the layout of the habitat. Even though Eastern Painted Turtles are solitary creatures by nature and frequently live alone in the wild, there are several circumstances in which introducing turtles may be required or preferred, such as in breeding programs or specific captive environments. We'll examine the factors, methods, and possible difficulties involved in socializing Eastern Painted Turtles in this investigation.

1. Getting to Know Eastern Painted Turtles' Social Behavior

Most people believe that eastern painted turtles are lonely creatures, and they rarely interact with other people in the wild. Males may, however, engage in courtship rituals throughout the mating season, and females may tolerate the company of other turtles under specific conditions. It is important to remember that every turtle has a unique temperament and set of preferences when thinking about introducing many turtles.

2. Appropriate Individuals for Socialization: Elements to Take into Account

Not every Eastern Painted Turtle is a good candidate for socializing. It is important to consider factors like sex, size, age, and temperament when assessing whether or not turtles can live in harmony with one another. Housing many males together is generally not advised since they may become territorial and violent, especially during breeding season. A higher likelihood of compatibility might be obtained by combining a male and female or several females.

3. Territorial Conduct: Reducing hostility

The social dynamics of Eastern Painted Turtles can be significantly influenced by territorial behavior. They mark territories in the wild, and habitats for captive turtles should allow enough room for each turtle to do so without being in continual rivalry with the others. Especially during breeding seasons, territorial violence might take the form of biting, chasing, or dominance-seeking behaviors.

4. Size Compatibility: Handling Disparities in Size

Take into account the variations in size between individual Eastern Painted Turtles when introducing many of them. Dominance problems can arise from huge size differences, when larger turtles may frighten or even hurt smaller ones. Seeing turtles with comparable sizes can lessen the possibility of hostility and foster a more harmonious group dynamic.

5. Designing a Habitat to Foster a Multi-Turtle Ecosystem
A key factor in successfully promoting socializing is the habitat's design. Make sure there are enough swimming spaces, hiding places, and basking locations in the habitat for turtles to be able to mark their individual territories. Visual barriers made of rocks, logs, and plants can lessen the likelihood of continuous visual contact, which can cause tension or hostility.

6. Keeping an Eye on Things and Evaluating Interactions
While first introducing Eastern Painted Turtles, careful observation is essential. Keep an eye out for indications of stress, aggression, or dominance in their interactions. Biting, chasing, altered basking behavior, and attempts

to monopolize resources are some examples of these symptoms. Should hostility arise, be ready to step in quickly to stop harm from happening.

7. Gradual Introduction: Give Yourself Some Time to Adjust

Turtles should be introduced gradually to reduce stress and aid in acclimation. Let them see each other without putting their bodies in direct contact to start. If at all possible, keep them apart at first with a barrier, like a clear divider. Gradually permit controlled interactions as they grow used to each other's company. This methodical approach lessens the possibility of confrontations turning violent.

8. Feeding Techniques: Diminishing Rivals

Turtles may compete with one another during feeding time. Make sure there are several feeding areas with enough room for each turtle to access food unhindered in order to reduce aggression. Until a steady feeding schedule is established, if necessary, keep a close eye on feeding interactions and think about separating turtles during meals.

9. Offering Hiding Places: Developing Retreat Choices
Include hiding places so that turtles can take refuge in the habitat when necessary. This is especially crucial if there is hostility since turtles can hide to decompress. Plants, artificial caves, or well-placed rocks can all act as hiding places and create a more peaceful atmosphere.

10. Divided Basking Areas: Preventing Territorial Wars
In order to avoid territorial disputes, it is crucial to provide distinct areas for basking, as Eastern Painted Turtles depend on this activity to regulate their body temperature. Because there are more floating areas, logs, or basking platforms available, each turtle can

select a spot without being crowded, which lowers the possibility of aggressive encounters during basking.

11. Gender Considerations: Behaviors Related to Mating and Breeding

Be ready for possible mating and breeding behaviors if you house male and female Eastern Painted Turtles together. Increased aggression may result from breeding, particularly if a female is unresponsive or if there is rivalry for her attention. If breeding is a factor, make sure the habitat has enough room for courtship rituals and nesting behaviors.

12. Possibilities for Nesting: Providing for Reproductive Habits

If there are female turtles around, make sure the habitat has enough places for them to nest. Even in captivity, females may engage in nest-building activities; providing a dedicated space with suitable material can assist in meeting their reproductive requirements. This can ease tension and lessen the possibility of disputes arising from nesting habits.

13. Compatibility Testing: New Addition Trial Times

Before allowing a new turtle to live permanently with the group, think about instituting trial periods. Start by introducing the new turtle to the habitat by setting it up in a different enclosure so the other turtles can get used to seeing it. Over time, progressively raise the degree of interaction while keeping an eye out for compatibility.

14. Procedures for Quarantine: Disease Prevention

Follow quarantine guidelines before adding a new turtle to an established group. For a while, keep the baby turtle alone to look for any indications of illness or disease. By taking this preventive measure, the health of all the resident turtles is protected from the possible spread of pathogens.

15. Veterinary Care: Consistent Evaluations of Health

All turtles in the habitat should have routine veterinary examinations scheduled, particularly when introducing new animals. Health evaluations can spot possible problems early on, such as symptoms of stress, wounds, or illnesses. Timely veterinary care is beneficial to the turtles' general health and makes socialization programs more effective.

16. Identifying Stress Signs and Taking Proactive Action

Stress symptoms could be displayed by Eastern Painted Turtles in reaction to alterations in their surroundings or interpersonal relationships. Common indicators include altered feeding habits, decreased activity, anomalies in the shell, or avoidance of the sun. Consider reevaluating the social dynamics, habitat design, or the necessity of individual housing if stress indicators are seen.

17. Individual Housing: Taking Into Account Everybody's Needs

Even with socialization efforts, solitary housing might be the best choice for some Eastern Painted Turtles. When kept with other turtles, certain turtles may exhibit signs of stress or hostility since they prefer to be alone. Recognize the unique requirements and habits of every turtle, and be ready to offer alternative housing if needed.

18. Adapting to Social Structures in Group Dynamics

Within a group, Eastern Painted Turtles can create a social hierarchy consisting of dominant and submissive individuals. In order to guarantee that all turtles have access to resources and can live in harmony with one another, it is crucial to acknowledge and adjust to these dynamics. If there is ongoing antagonism, step in and, if needed, think about changing the makeup of the group.

19. Enhancing the Environment through Invigorating Activities

Incorporate activities that enrich the environment to improve the socializing process. Turtles need mental and physical stimulation, and you may make their environment more interesting and active by offering them new things, changing up their habitat, or adding live food.

20. Socialization Success: Tracking Harmony Over Time

Effective socialization is a lifelong process that necessitates constant observation of both individual and group actions. With careful maintenance, frequent observation, and habitat modifications based on the changing requirements and interactions of Eastern Painted Turtles, long-term harmony can be attained.

In conclusion, creating environments that are harmonious

It takes a sophisticated grasp of Eastern Painted Turtle behavior, individual personalities, and environmental dynamics to successfully socialize them. Careful planning, moderate introductions, and vigilant monitoring are necessary to create a harmonious ecosystem and guarantee each turtle's well-being. Even while certain turtles could do better in a social environment, it's important to recognize and honor each turtle's preferences and give them the choice of private housing when necessary. Turtle lovers may improve the health and richness of their Eastern Painted Turtle friends by creating an atmosphere that supports social interactions as well as individual requirements.

FAQs

What is the Eastern Painted Turtle's scientific name?

A: Chrysemys picta picta is the scientific name for the Eastern Painted Turtle.

What is the average adult Eastern Painted Turtle's size?

A: The carapace length of an adult Eastern Painted Turtle typically ranges from 4 to 10 inches.

How can I tell the difference between Eastern Painted Turtles, males and females?

A: Compared to females, male Eastern Painted Turtles typically have longer, thicker tails. Generally speaking, females are bigger.

How long does an Eastern Painted Turtle live in captivity?

A: Eastern Painted Turtles can survive for several decades in captivity; their lifespans can reach 40 years or longer.

In the wild, what kind of habitat do Eastern Painted Turtles prefer?

A: Ponds, lakes, marshes, and meandering streams are among the watery settings that Eastern Painted Turtles call home.

Is it possible for me to have a pet Eastern Painted Turtle?

A good habitat and adequate care are essential for Eastern Painted Turtles, however they are widely kept as pets.

In the wild, what do Eastern Painted Turtles eat?

A variety of aquatic vegetation, insects, tiny fish, crabs, and even carrion are part of its diet.

What kind of food is best for an Eastern Painted Turtle kept as a pet?

A well-rounded diet for Eastern Painted Turtles kept as pets should consist of commercial turtle pellets, veggies, leafy greens, and occasionally treats like frozen or live prey.

What's the ideal feeding schedule for an Eastern Painted Turtle?

A: Adult Eastern Painted Turtles should be fed two to three times a week; baby turtles might need to be fed every day.

Do Eastern Painted Turtles get enough sun exposure outside of the water?

A: In order to control their body temperature, Eastern Painted Turtles do indeed bask. Assign a heat source to a basking area.

What is the Eastern Painted Turtle's preferred water temperature?

A: To protect Eastern Painted Turtles, keep the water temperature between 75 and 85°F (24 and 29°C).

Do Eastern Painted Turtles hibernate over the colder months?

A: It is true that throughout the winter, Eastern Painted Turtles hibernate, frequently burying themselves in mud at the bottom of water bodies.

How can I provide my Eastern Painted Turtle with a suitable basking area?

A: Give them access to a dry place with a heat lamp or basking light and a smooth rock or platform to climb on.

Can Eastern Painted Turtles live among other types of turtles?

A: Keeping different species of turtles in the same enclosure is usually not advised because of the possibility of territorial behavior.

Are Eastern Painted Turtles suitable for novice turtle keepers?

A: Yes, because of their resilience and flexibility, Eastern Painted Turtles are frequently suggested for novices.

How Do Eastern Painted Turtles Interact with Each Other?

A: Eastern Painted Turtles use their head bobbing, swimming patterns, and tactile interactions as forms of body language to communicate.

Do Eastern Painted Turtles migrate during the day or at night?

A: Eastern Painted Turtles are mostly active during the day, as they are diurnal creatures.

How are eggs laid by Eastern Painted Turtles?

A: The females lay their eggs in soft or sandy soil through internal fertilization.

What is the number of eggs laid in a clutch by an Eastern Painted Turtle?

A typical clutch size might vary from two to twenty eggs, contingent upon the size and age of the female.

What is the duration of incubation for eggs laid by Eastern Painted Turtles?

A: The temperature affects the gender of the hatchlings during the 60–90 day incubation period.

Is it possible to provide my Eastern Painted Turtle a floating platform to lounge on?

A: Certainly, providing easy access to dry regions, a floating basking platform can be a useful addition to the habitat.

Do Eastern Painted Turtles know who owns them?

A: They might grow acclimated to their owners' presence and identify them with food, even though they are not known for having good recognition.

Can I have more than one Eastern Painted Turtle in my home?

A: You can house more than one Eastern Painted Turtle together, but keep an eye out for any signs of stress or violence.

Is UVB illumination necessary for Eastern Painted Turtles?

A: In order for Eastern Painted Turtles to process calcium and preserve the health of their shells, UVB lighting is necessary.

Is it possible for me to provide my Eastern Painted Turtle an enclosure with a heat mat?

A: Heat mats can be utilized, but it's important to make sure they don't burn people or overheat the habitat.

Do Eastern Painted Turtles have good swimming abilities?

A: It is true that Eastern Painted Turtles spend a lot of time in the water and are proficient swimmers.

Are fruits safe for Eastern Painted Turtles to eat?

A: Because of their high sugar content, fruits should not constitute a substantial component of their diet, but they can be given on occasion.

Do Scutes Come Off in Eastern Painted Turtles?

A: Scutes do shed from Eastern Painted Turtles as they mature. Establish a suitable basking space to promote healthy shedding.

I have an Eastern Painted Turtle. Can I handle it frequently?

A: Although some people can handle, too much handling can be stressful. Handle only what is absolutely essential, such as health examinations.

What is the typical range of temperatures in Eastern Painted Turtles' natural habitat?

A temperate environment is their usual home, though they can be found in a variety of temperature ranges in their native habitat.

Do predators exist for Eastern Painted Turtles in the wild?

A: Predators do exist; they include birds, larger turtles, raccoons, and occasionally fish.

How can I give my Eastern Painted Turtle more environmental enrichment?

A: To encourage their natural habits, enrichment can include a range of tank décor, live plants, and puzzle feeders.

What symptoms indicate a disease in Eastern Painted Turtles?

A: Swelling eyes, irregular swimming patterns, anomalies in the shell, lethargy, and changes in appetite are among the symptoms.

Is it possible for Eastern Painted Turtles to only consume commercial turtle pellets?

A diversified diet including vegetables, greens, and occasionally live or frozen prey is advised, even though pellets are a staple.

What are the signs of dehydration in an Eastern Painted Turtle?

A: Sunken eyes, sluggishness, dry or flaky skin, and a lack of appetite are symptoms of dehydration.

Can brackish water affect Eastern Painted Turtles?

A: No, brackish water is not a suitable habitat for Eastern Painted Turtles, as they are freshwater creatures.

Are Eastern Painted Turtles able to speak or produce noises?

A: No, Eastern Painted Turtles don't usually talk or make noise.

What is the best way to furnish my Eastern Painted Turtle with a naturalistic habitat?

A: To replicate their natural habitat, use rocks, natural substrate, and live or silk plants.

Is it possible to keep Eastern Painted Turtles in outdoor ponds?

A natural environment can be provided by keeping them in outside ponds, provided that the temperature is adequate for doing so.

Is a water filter necessary for Eastern Painted Turtles?

A: In order to keep water clean by eliminating contaminants and waste, a water filter is necessary.

Can Eastern Painted Turtles generate new shells if they are damaged?

A: As they cannot regenerate new shells like certain other turtles, it is important to keep them from becoming hurt.

Can fish be kept in the same home as Eastern Painted Turtles?

A: Although certain fish might get along, care must be taken because some might bite the turtle in the limbs.

Are Eastern Painted Turtles Color-Recognizant?

A: They haven't been researched too much, although they can tell the difference between light and dark, and they might be drawn to particular hues.

Is a substrate necessary for Eastern Painted Turtles in their tank?

A: A substrate such as smooth gravel or sand can improve the looks of the tank, but it's not required.

Can earthworms be consumed by Eastern Painted Turtles?

A: They can incorporate earthworms in their diet as they are a nutrient-dense food source.

Is it permissible to own Eastern Painted Turtles as pets everywhere?

A: Verify local laws regarding pet ownership, as they may differ.

Can Painted Turtles in the East Climb?

A: Since they are not skilled climbers, offer low, accessible areas for them to sunbathe.

Can groups of Eastern Painted Turtles coexist?

A: They can live together, but keep an eye out for aggressive behavior, particularly when they're feeding.

Do captive Eastern Painted Turtles hibernate?

A: Although hibernation may not be required in captivity, some owners choose to simulate winter circumstances in order to promote reproduction.

What can I do to help preserve Eastern Painted Turtles in their natural habitat?

A: Donate to conservation groups, adopt moral pet ownership guidelines, and stay away from buying turtles from shady or illegal sources.